The Grief Revolution respectfully acknowledges the Traditional Owners and Custodians of the lands on which we live and work. Paying our respects to Elders, past, present and emerging, and extend this acknowledgement to all Aboriginal and Torres Strait Islander Peoples across the nation who continue to care for their Country, culture and people.

Hi friend

First Edition January 2024

Hi friend

ABN 23365422443

National Library of Australia

Cataloguing-in-Publication entry

ISBN/SKU 9780645298703

For Rick, my friend, my father and my forever teacher.

Life, birth and death are beautiful and sacred.
You are invited to find that beauty...

THE
grief
REVOLUTION

www.thegriefrevolution.com.au
www.instagram.com/the_grief_revolution

Hi Friend!

I am Sophie Mills, and I am so excited you have chosen to read this beautiful book with a child in your life.

I am an Occupational Therapist who specialises in emotional literacy and death education.

As the founder of The Grief Revolution, I help caregivers demystify the scary and taboo topics of grief and death with the children in their life. Together we can revolutionise this silence culture we find ourselves in.

Let's move away from viewing grief and death as unthinkable, unspeakable or even offensive, and instead, find deep gratitude for our ability to experience consciousness in human form.

Let's learn to bask in the full sensory and emotional experiences that living offers, and return to honouring death as the sacred and beautiful gift that it is.

For engaging, educational and chucklesome content, follow me on socials at www.instagram.com/the_grief_revolution

A message to parents, educators and other caregivers

Thank you for reading this book with a child in your life, and thank you for your willingness to engage with a topic that can feel uncomfortable. Fear and discomfort surrounding grief and death is a normal outcome of cultural conditioning. This conditioning has seen a huge censoring of information with the hope to "protect" children.

Adhering to the current silence culture leaves children feeling unable to ask questions which can cause much confusion.

Children are left to piece together fragments of information, often resulting in unhealthy, fear-based conclusions. We now know that providing children with factual and age-appropriate information, allows them to form a healthy relationship with mortality, free from fear and confusion.

When talking to your children about grief and death please know:

-You do not have to know all the answers. It is perfectly acceptable and in fact encouraged to offer "I don't know, what do you think?"

-You do not need to explain everything at once. Pause often and wait for your child to guide the conversation through their questions.

-Language is important. Using the terms dead, died and death are necessary to use over "went to sleep", "are in a better place", "lost/resting" and the like.

-Reassure your child that they will always be loved and cared for, validate their fears, and allow any emotions that arise.

-Crying is a very normal and healthy response to learning of the mortality of all living things. Remain fully present with your child, without silencing or distracting them as they process the emotions.

-You will likely see themes surrounding death arise in your child/ren's play. This is a healthy way of processing the new information and is perfectly normal and acceptable. Allow this type of play so long as all involved are safe.

-The stories you tell your children become their inner dialogue and have a major impact on how they view the world. Being truthful and vulnerable with your children about your own personal experiences will provide an example of what healthy grieving looks like. By doing this, you give the child permission to cry and talk about their own experience, both now and in the future.

-Children are talented observers. Your body language, facial expressions and unspoken words are all communicating a message. If you feel you are communicating a message that is not aligned with the above recommendations, you are likely a part of the majority of adults who experience death anxiety or discomfort. It can be useful to become curious about the fear you hold surrounding death and implement strategies to address these fears.

After addressing their own fears, parents have reported they were able to more comfortably and confidently talk to their children about grief and death, as well as better support their children through any fears or emotions that arose.

Hi Friend.

Creating open conversations with children about grief and death

Written by
Sophie Mills

Illustrated by
Marina Regali

Edited by
Brand Artisians Australia

THE grief REVOLUTION

The Grief Revolution

"Mum, ever since the neighbour's rabbit died, I'm worried that Flopsy will die too," said Zoe.

"I can see how that would make you feel worried," Mum replied.
"It's hard not knowing when someone or something we love will die."

"How about I introduce you to some friends who have had a loved one die? We might learn something from their experiences," suggested Zoe's Mum.

Hi Friend, I'm Cooper!

This is my mummy. A few years ago, she said a baby was going to join our family. I was so excited!

Weeks later, I saw mummy crying in the shower.

She told me that she was upset because her baby died, and that we wouldn't be meeting them anymore.

I could feel the sadness surrounding Mummy and Daddy.

They seemed to find comfort in extra cuddles with each other,
and since I felt sad too, they let me join in.

That night, we lit a candle to honour our angel baby
that left my mummy's womb.

After hearing Cooper's story, Zoe turned to her mother and asked,
"could we light a candle when Flopsy dies too, Mum?"

Hi Friend, I'm Lily!

"What a beautiful idea," Zoe's Mum replied.
"You know, there are other ways we can honour those who have died.
I have a special someone who can tell you about it."

A few years ago, my grandma told me she had something called cancer.

After that, she couldn't play with me as much.
She said her body felt really tired.

My grandma then moved into our house, and later on,
she stopped being able to get out of bed.

One day, she smiled at me for the last time
before her body stopped working and she died.

We cared for Grandma's body at home for a few days,
washing her skin and rubbing her favourite cream and oils into it.

Mum said this was a loving way to honour Grandma
for being a beautiful light in our life.

The next day my Grandma's body was taken to the crematorium.
I felt kind of heavy. I was starting to really miss playing with Grandma each day.
My dad cuddled me and said that I was forever loved and always protected.

Mum said even though we won't ever see Grandma's body again,
we were always connected through our deep and never ending love.

Zoe looked to her Mum and asked, "Mum, will I feel sad when Flopsy dies?"
"You will at times, not always," Zoe's Mum replied.

Hi Friend, I'm Tully!

"Sometimes you will feel heavy and sad because you miss her, other times
you will feel warm and happy because you got to love her. When someone dies,
we hold a special event to celebrate that love.
It is called a funeral.
I have another friend that can tell you about his sister's funeral."

My sister and I, used to do everything together.
She was my best friend and I loved her with my whole heart.

One day, my dad told me that my sister got badly hurt
and we had to go straight to hospital to get her help.

After a few hours, a doctor came to tell us that Mia died.
We went in to see her body,
and my Dads held her and cried for a really long time. I cried too.

A week later we went to Mia's funeral. It was at a park and we got her a cardboard coffin that we all spent the day decorating. I wished Mia was there to hold my hand, but Dad said once someone dies, they don't ever come back.
That hurt my heart.

I did like having all my cousins together at the funeral. They are really funny.

I liked the game we played where we killed the dragon who hurt our Mia.

Zoe turned to her mother and asked, "could we have a funeral for Flopsy when she dies Mum?"

"Sure, your cousins could come and help dig the hole to place Flopsy . They could help gather flowers and leaves to put on top after we cover her with dirt too," Zoe's Mum replied.
"I'd like that, agreed Zoe".

Ever since my grandma left her body,
I've come to see death as a beautiful rite of passage.
It doesn't mean I don't miss her and feel sad about it,
it just means I also feel joy and love.

Before my grandma died, she told me that when I'm having a tough time,
I can do dinosaur roars to help get the emotions out of my body.
I've still got Grandma's pillow which I use for pillow fights
with Mum and Dad too.

I made a new friend called Tully. He lives on my street.
His sister died, so he knows how it feels to lose someone close.
Tully comes to our house a lot, and my dad
puts on the best puppet shows for us.

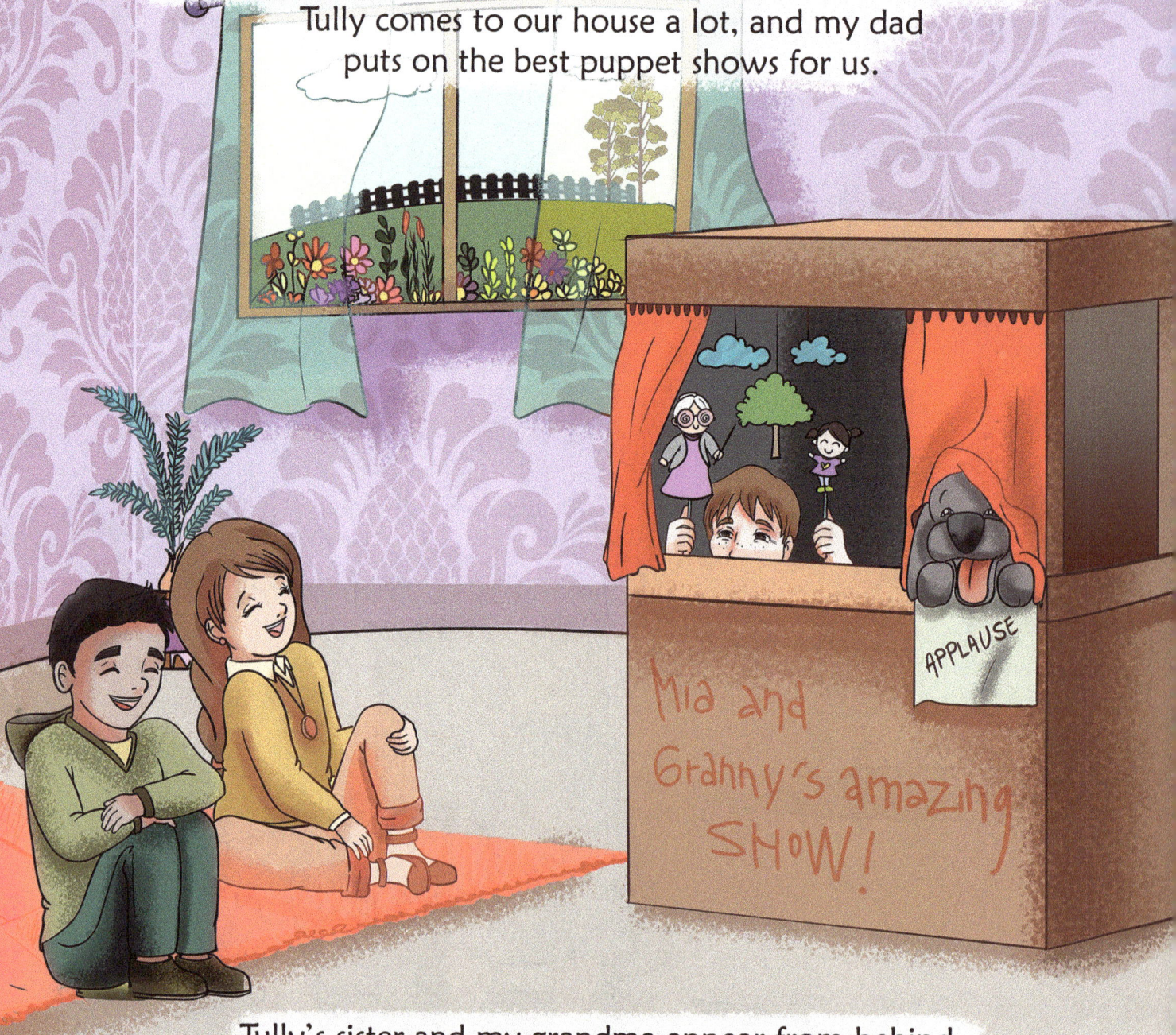

APPLAUSE

Mia and
Granny's amazing
SHOW!

Tully's sister and my grandma appear from behind
the red curtain and make us laugh so much.

It's been years since my sister, Mia, died and
my heart is still hurting, but it is healing.
We talk about Mia every day still.

Dad says I'm going to miss her forever,
and that it's okay to still feel really sad.

I've learned so much since Mia died, especially about butterflies.

Butterflies live for about a month, unless
they get very, very sick, or badly hurt.
Like what happened to my Mia.

If a butterfly doesn't get better from the hurt or sickness, they die.
That can happen if they are young or old, because nothing can live forever.
My dad tells me it isn't anyone's fault when someone or something dies.

Mum turned to Zoe and asked, "did you know, sometimes a butterfly is gifted to a mother when her baby dies? It is given as a mark of remembrance."

Hi again, Friend!
- Cooper

"Was Cooper's Mum gifted a butterfly then?" Zoe asked.
"I'm not sure, let's find out," Zoe's Mum replied.

It's been a year since Mummy's baby left her womb.
Today my mummy birthed her rainbow baby in a pool at home.
I was right there to see Finn take his first breath.

Mummy says Finn wouldn't be here if our angel baby didn't die,
so we find ways to show our gratitude for that.

We even included Mummy's butterfly
in our first family photo, to honour the baby we never met.

We still light a candle for our angel baby each year too.

"So, Cooper's Mum was gifted a butterfly!" said Zoe.
"Now you see Zoe," said Mum, "that death is a natural part of life,
but with it, comes big emotions.
When Flopsy dies, all those who care for
you will come to support and love you,
helping you to heal your heart."

"I love you Mum, and I love you Flopsy,"
replied Zoe hugging Flopsy before she hopped away.

www.ingramcontent.com/pod-product-compliance
Lightning Source LLC
Chambersburg PA
CBHW062007090426
42811CB00005B/776

* 9 7 8 0 6 4 5 2 9 8 7 0 3 *